Easter
PROGRAMS
for the CHURCH

compiled by

Pat Fittro

Standard
PUBLISHING
CINCINNATI, OHIO

Standard Publishing, Cincinnati, Ohio
A division of Standex International Corporation
© 2002 by Standard Publishing

ISBN 0-7847-1297-2

Contents

The Weaver's Apprentice
Judy A. Land

Hebrews 9, 10 and 1 Chronicles 16:29

Synopsis: Jacob, a young devout Jew, is an apprentice to Hosea the weaver. Hosea is a Levite working on the replacement of the Veil to the Most Holy Place.[1] Jacob's father, a Pharisee, talks of the new Teacher at the temple who "seems to cast out demons by the Prince of demons." When the Veil to the Most Holy Place is rent from top to bottom, Jacob is filled with wonder. The risen Christ appears in the last scene to explain (from Hebrews 9, 10) that He is the new High Priest, and His body, as the curtain, was torn to provide access to the throne of God.

Characters:
JACOB: Apprentice at a fabric store, 15-25 years old, devout Jew
CLEOPAS: Jacob's father, a Pharisee, haughty
HOSEA: Levite, older man, the weaver who is training Jacob
DEMETRIUS: Blind man who runs errands for Hosea, healed by Jesus
CUSTOMERS at fabric shop: five or six women
JESUS: Seen only in last scene
LEAH: A little younger than Jacob, Demetrius's sister who was demon-possessed and healed by Jesus
CHOIR: Optional

Props: For Hosea's weaving shop—
Fabric: upholstery, linens, burlap, velvet solids, no lace or cotton/polyester; folded up and placed on floor or tables
Table with wooden box, yellow construction paper with torn edges to look like papyrus, quill and inkwell (Don't fill with real ink!)
Spindles, made with dowels or wire whisks
Wooden stool, broom
"Open" and "Closed" sign for door
Curtain exit for weaver's room at back of shop

---

[1] Edersheim, *Life and Times of Jesus the Messiah*, Chapter XV, p. 611.

Costumes:

Cleopas: Cleopas is a Pharisee. Use white, purple, and/or embroidered linen for upper garments, with blue fringes on the borders. The inner garment should go down to the heels. The headdress consists of a pointed cap, or kind of turban, of satin or shiny polyester.

Hosea: Traditional Jewish costume of Jesus' time, with apron or sash with pockets for spindles and spools

Jacob, Demetrius, Leah, and Customers: Traditional Jewish costume of Jesus' time. Demetrius wears a cloth over his eyes and carries a cane.

Outline:

Scene I: I AM, the Teacher

"Open" sign on the window is facing the inside of the room, hence the store is closed, but Hosea is straightening piles of cloth and spools of thread. He has a spindle stuck behind his ear, as a person would hold a pencil in modern times, and he is mumbling to himself. Once the store is open and throughout the scene, women come into the shop and browse. Some of them purchase items and some of them leave empty-handed. There is a knock at the door and Jacob enters.

HOSEA: Ah. You must be the new apprentice!

JACOB *(as the two shake hands):* Yes Sir. Jacob, son of Cleopas, Sir.

HOSEA *(rubbing his chin as if thinking):* Son of Cleopas, son of Cleopas . . . Cleopas the Pharisee?

JACOB: Well, yes, Sir.

HOSEA: I know him well. Good man. See him at the temple all the time. He does know his Scriptures, doesn't he?

JACOB: Yes, he does, Sir.

HOSEA: Well, let's get busy. These are the fabrics we've ordered from parts of Judea *(waving arm at a stack of fabric)*, and those over there *(pointing elsewhere at a stack of fabric)* were made by a woman named Lydia, and here *(handling some fabric)* are some I've woven myself. What you'll be doing is helping me keep track of orders and selling and also doing some weaving. You are a Levite, are you not?

JACOB: Yes, Sir.

HOSEA: That's what I thought. And that's why I chose you, Jacob. As you probably know, we are constantly working on replacing veils for the temple and each year we replace two of them. To keep them looking nice and new, you know. *(Jacob nods.)* This year, I've chosen to work on the Veil to the Most Holy Place. It's the thickest and largest of the thirteen veils in the temple. Twenty-four cords are woven together first and then each plait of twenty-four is woven with seventy-two other plaits to form the huge curtain that separates the Holy Place from the Most Holy Place.[2] *(Jacob whistles or says, "Whoa.")* It's an awesome responsibility and that's why I've hired you to help out here and sometimes back in the weaving room.

JACOB *(respectfully):* Yes, Sir.

HOSEA: Good. *(Slaps him on the back.)* I'm sure I can trust you to do the job. We'll probably have another busy day today. Better go ahead and turn the sign around. *(Indicates the sign on the window.)* I'll be working in the back. *(Leaves through curtain to back room.)*

(Jacob turns the sign around so "closed" shows on the inside of the room. Three women walk through the open doorway. Two of them look at various articles for sale, picking up cloth to inspect. Jacob shows them fabric, spindles, or thread, and takes their coins to the cash box as they purchase items. The third woman is describing to Jacob a curtain she would like to have made. He gets out a book or scroll, and makes notations on a piece of papyrus with a quill dipped in an inkwell. In the middle of the exchanges, Cleopas walks in and approaches Jacob. The customer finishes her order and exits the shop.)

CLEOPAS *(putting his arm around Jacob's shoulders proudly):* Well, Son, how's the new job going?

JACOB: Father, I only just started.

---

[2] ibid, Chapter XV, p. 611

CLEOPAS *(looking around curiously):* Of course, of course. Well, I was on my way to the temple to get the Passover lamb inspected and just thought I'd stop by.

(Demetrius walks in.)

DEMETRIUS: Hosea?

(Jacob goes forward to help the blind man. Cleopas shrinks back to avoid touching Demetrius.)

JACOB: Shalom, Demetrius! This is Jacob! Hosea is in the back room.
DEMETRIUS: Jacob! I knew Hosea was going to hire you. Glad to find you here. Before you take me back, though, tell me this: Have you heard the new Teacher at the temple?
JACOB *(glancing at his father uncomfortably):* Uh, not exactly.
CLEOPAS *(authoritatively):* Shalom, Demetrius.
DEMETRIUS *(unenthusiastically, disappointed):* Oh, shalom, Cleopas.
CLEOPAS: You speak of Jesus of Nazareth. *(With disdain.)* Goes around saying things like, "I am the light of the world." What is that supposed to mean? Have you heard Him talk?
DEMETRIUS: Of course I've heard Him talk. And I believe in Him.
CLEOPAS *(with scorn):* Surely your ears aren't as dead as your eyes, brother Demetrius.
JACOB *(shocked):* Father!
CLEOPAS: I'm sorry. I shouldn't have said that. But really, the Man makes the most ludicrous claims—He not only claims to be sent from Heaven by His Father, God; He tells the rest of us that we don't even know God! Imagine, talking to the learned rabbis like that!
DEMETRIUS *(sarcastically):* Yes, imagine.
JACOB: Well, why don't you just kick Him out of the temple, Father?
CLEOPAS: We can't, because of the people. He has a huge following. *(Looks around to make sure no one is listening, leans closer to Jacob's ear.)* He told me I was of my father the devil! Me—a Levite! *(Shakes his head, incredulous.)* The words still ring in my ears.

(Demetrius smiles broadly but says nothing.)

JACOB: He actually said that?

CLEOPAS: Sure, and more. Lots more. A schlemiel *(pronounced "shleh-meel")* from Galilee, that's what He is. Goes around quoting the Law and the prophets like He wrote the Scriptures himself! Why, He even said He knew Abraham! Said He was born before Abraham, in fact! *(Pause.)*

JACOB *(wipes his forehead in amazement):* Whew!

CLEOPAS *(glances back and forth again dramatically):* I don't want to be overheard in here, Jacob *(ignoring Demetrius),* but He claimed to be I AM! The name God gave to Moses . . . Tell the people "I AM hath sent me unto you,"[3] if you remember the Scripture, Jacob.

JACOB *(thoughtfully):* Well that is something to consider.

(Customers begin to leave one by one.)

DEMETRIUS *(loudly, obviously wishing to embarrass Cleopas):* I AM!? He said He was I AM, brother Cleopas?

CLEOPAS *(straightens up and glares at Demetrius):* Yes, Demetrius, and I'd appreciate it if you'd keep your voice down when speaking of these matters.

DEMETRIUS: Why?

CLEOPAS: You'll see. Followers of this Jesus fellow may have to watch themselves one day. He's nothing but trouble.

JACOB: But, could He be—*(pause, then, almost in a whisper)* Could He really be the Mess—

DEMETRIUS *(again, loudly):* The Messiah?

CLEOPAS *(angrily):* No! A thousand times no! Don't even think it! The whole Sanhedrin agrees. There is no way this Man can be the Messiah. *(Waves as if to dismiss the subject.)* Well, enough of this talk.

(Customers have all left by now.)

DEMETRIUS: Come, take a poor blind man to the weaver's room, good Jacob. *(Holds his elbow out for Jacob to take, then waves toward Cleopas.)* Shalom, misguided Pharisee!

---

[3] Exodus 3:14, *KJV*

(Jacob leads Demetrius toward weaver's room.)

CLEOPAS *(having started to give a salutation, hears the "misguided Pharisee" remark and changes his mind, turns on his heel haughtily and walks toward the door):* I'll see you this evening, Jacob. *(Leaves through door. Jacob and Demetrius leave through weaver's curtain.)*

CHOIR: "I Am" *(Words by Wayne Hilliard, music by Michael Smith, arranged by Ferrin.)*

Scene II: I AM, the Healer

Hosea and Jacob are sweeping and straightening shelves again at the beginning of another workday. Jacob turns the "Open" sign over and opens the door to customers. Several customers come in and purchase fabric or pick up finished curtains or blankets and pay for them, then leave the store. No dialogue but instrumental version of an Easter song of your choice is heard. Customers have left and store is empty except for Hosea and Jacob.

HOSEA: So, Jacob, how's your Passover lamb doing?

JACOB: Oh, you mean Blackey?

HOSEA: You named it?

JACOB *(laughs):* My brother Caleb named it. He's only five and he gets very attached to animals.

HOSEA: Ah, I remember those days! I used to get attached to the Passover lambs myself. Is Caleb the one who asks the questions at the table when you have your Unleavened Bread meal, then?

JACOB: Ah, yes. He's been practicing with my sister. It's kind of comical, but I think he'll get it down.

HOSEA: It doesn't matter if he doesn't get it right. Your father will instruct all of you in the proper way to eat the meal and hear about the history of our people. Your father is a good man, very learned in the books of the Law. He has trained you well, Jacob. *(Sighs.)* I suppose he told you all about what happened at the temple yesterday.

JACOB: He had a meeting last night with the Sanhedrin and I didn't get to talk to him after dinner. What happened?

HOSEA: Well, that Jesus fellow came in, saw all the commerce that was going on, and proceeded to throw everybody out.

JACOB: He threw them out?

HOSEA: I was there myself, helping in one of the money-changing booths. He was very angry! He grabbed a whip from one of the servants who was there guarding the money, started whirling it around, turning over the tables, shouting at us. It was horrible! There were doves flying here and there from cages that had been overturned, a few lambs were running around loose, and coins flew everywhere! I couldn't believe my eyes! You know, Jacob, this is getting serious. We need to get rid of this Man before the Feast of Unleavened Bread and Passover Week. We can't have Him upsetting the people during these holy days. It's an outrage. You won't believe what He said.

JACOB: What?

HOSEA: He said, "It is written, My house shall be called the house of prayer; but ye have made it a den of thieves."[4] Imagine the chutzpah, saying something like that. He practically claimed the temple was His own house, which insinuates, once again, that He is God. We've just got to get rid of that Man. Your father would agree with me on this one. He's dangerous.

(Jacob shakes his head. A customer comes into the shop and the discussion ends.)

HOSEA: I need to take care of some things at home, Jacob. Keep an eye on the store and I'll be back in a few hours.

(Jacob nods. The customer leaves, and Jacob sits on a stool working on making a spindle. One or two customers walk in and quietly inspect cloth at one end of the shop. Jacob is humming, "King of Kings and Lord of Lords." Demetrius bursts in, wearing a big grin and full of excitement, but still wearing the cloth over his eyes. As

---

[4] Matthew 21:13, *KJV*

Demetrius speaks and dances around excitedly, the customers glance over their shoulders at him curiously.)

JACOB: Demetrius, shalom. What's all the excitement?

DEMETRIUS: Shalom, dear little brother. Guess what?

JACOB *(sulkily):* I hate it when people say, "Guess what?" Just tell me.

DEMETRIUS: You know my sister Leah, who has had a demon for seven years and stays in the house moaning all day and never combs her hair?

JACOB *(skeptically and slowly):* Ye-es.

DEMETRIUS *(beaming):* She's been healed!

JACOB: What do you mean, she's been healed?

DEMETRIUS: Healed. Well. No longer sick. Healthy. Demon-free. Hallelujah! *(Skips around in a circle laughing.)* Praise the Lord, my sister is healed! What more can the Creator do? Hallelujah!

JACOB *(skeptically):* Leah?

DEMETRIUS: Yes! Yes! Leah! Who was formerly demon-possessed, drooling, clawing at herself, sitting naked in a corner of—

JACOB: All right, all right! Who did this?

DEMETRIUS: Jesus of Nazareth, Son of God.

JACOB: What? Listen, Demetrius—and quit that dancing. *(Looks around.)* You're frightening the customers. My father says Jesus casts out demons by the Prince of demons!

DEMETRIUS: He did?

JACOB: Yes!

DEMETRIUS: Well, I say your father is a big schlemiel! Ha-ha!

JACOB: What? Hey, stop that! *(Steps off stool temporarily to steady Demetrius, who is still dancing.)* Somebody's going to hear you! Your sister probably just decided to comb her hair for a change. Now just settle down and let's talk rationally. *(Sits back on stool.)*

DEMETRIUS: I can't settle down. I won't settle down. *(Pause.)* Want to know why?

JACOB: Why?

DEMETRIUS *(fairly bursting with excitement):* That's not all Jesus did.

JACOB *(frowning, doubtful):* What else did He do?

DEMETRIUS *(dramatically rips off the cloth that covered his eyes):* Look!

JACOB *(gasps):* Put that thing back on.

DEMETRIUS: No! No! I can see! I was blind, but now I see! He healed me too!

(Jacob, formerly sitting on a stool, stands up.)

JACOB: You can see?

DEMETRIUS: Plain as day. I'll prove it. *(Points to Jacob.)* You, Sir, are ugly! Ha! Ha!

JACOB *(frowning):* What expression do I have on my face right now?

DEMETRIUS: Easy. Bewilderment.

JACOB: How about now? *(Puts his thumbs in his ears and wiggles his fingers. Demetrius also puts his thumbs in his ears and wiggles his fingers to mimic Jacob. As soon as he does this, Jacob steps back and shouts—AUGH—as if he has seen a ghost.)* You can see!

DEMETRIUS: Praise be to the God of Abraham, Isaac, and Jacob, yes! I can see, I can see, I can see! Jacob! Look over there. *(Points behind Jacob.)* I can't believe what I am seeing. *(Jacob turns to look, but sees nothing behind him.)* Ha! Ha! Made you look! *(Jacob smiles.)*

JACOB *(smiling and shaking his head):* I just can't believe it. My father says this Jesus is—

DEMETRIUS: Jesus is the Messiah, the Son of God. Only God could do this, Jacob. Believe and be free!

JACOB *(shaking his head):* I—I guess I really do believe, Demetrius. But I have to honor my father. He is so strongly against Jesus, I—I just don't know what to say or what to think. If . . . if I could only talk to Jesus, face to face . . . to see what He is really like.

DEMETRIUS: Your father and the Sanhedrin don't like Jesus because He says He is God's Son, sent from Heaven to redeem mortal man. He is the Messiah. The Pharisees don't want someone coming here and being the Messiah. They are used to being in charge themselves.

JACOB: That's not true! You speak blasphemy!

DEMETRIUS: No, Jacob. It is Cleopas and the nonbelieving Jews who speak blasphemy. You will understand one day, my brother. *(Pats him on the back.)* You'll see, as I do. Not only with my eyes, but with my heart. *(Sighs.)* Oh, Jacob, it is so good to see the sun! And good to see the Son of God, too!

12

JACOB: I'm glad for you, Demetrius. And for your sister too.

DEMETRIUS: Thank you, my little brother. Shalom! *(Exits out door.)*

JACOB: Shalom!

CHOIR: "It Took a Miracle" *(by John Peterson, or your choice)*

Scene III: I AM, the Veil

Jacob, alone in the fabric shop, is sweeping the floor. It has been four days since the crucifixion. He whistles or hums a Jewish tune. After straightening the shelves and looking out the window, he changes the sign to read "open" and opens the door. Then he sits on the wooden stool and picks up some papyrus papers with notes on them, checking the figures against the cash box. Demetrius and his sister walk in. Demetrius is excited and his sister is embarrassed and shy.

DEMETRIUS: Shalom, brother!

JACOB: Shalom! *(Stares at Leah.)* Is that—

DEMETRIUS: You remember my little sister Leah, don't you Jacob?

LEAH *(shyly):* Shalom.

JACOB *(still staring):* Is it really you? *(Stumbling over the words.)* Shalom! Well, hi! Hello. Shalom. Leah, you surely look different.

LEAH: Jesus cast out the demon.

JACOB *(still staring):* Unbelievable. I mean, I know.

DEMETRIUS: Quite an improvement, eh Jacob?

JACOB *(still staring):* Uh-huh.

DEMETRIUS: You feeling all right, Jacob?

JACOB *(shaking his head):* Oh, sorry. It's just that she looks so—

LEAH: Human?

JACOB: Well, you looked pretty bad before. *(Then, hastily.)* No—I didn't mean that!

LEAH: No. It's all right.

JACOB: Anyway, you look better now. I mean—your hair looks nice.

LEAH *(reaching up to touch her hair):* Thank you.

DEMETRIUS *(clearing his throat):* Is Hosea here?

JACOB *(still staring at Leah):* No. Hasn't come in yet. *(Then looking at Demetrius who has walked toward the curtain to the back room.)* Hey, where are you going?

DEMETRIUS: Just thought I'd glance at the Veil again. *(Opens the curtain to the back room and glances inside, then closes it and returns to the room.)* A magnificent piece of work, is it not, to shield man from the presence of God himself in the temple? I wonder . . . *(Rubs his chin as if in thought, then, clearing his mind to the present.)* So, you haven't seen Hosea since the night of the crucifixion?

JACOB *(turning to walk toward Demetrius):* No. Why?

DEMETRIUS: The Veil in the temple was rent in two.

JACOB: What? Which Veil?

DEMETRIUS: The big one. The one Hosea's been working on replacing. *(Pointing to the back room.)* It is the Veil that separates the Holy Place from the Most Holy Place.

JACOB: That impossible. *(Looks from Demetrius to Leah and back again.)*

DEMETRIUS: I heard it just this morning. The priests were offering the evening sacrifice of incense just as Jesus was being crucified, and the Veil just ripped from top to bottom in front of their faces.

JACOB *(disbelieving):* Who told you this?

DEMETRIUS: The priests! Hasn't your father heard about it?

JACOB: He hasn't said anything, but I'm sure he'll have an explanation.

DEMETRIUS: And a Scripture verse or two to quote.

JACOB: This is crazy. The curtain was a handbreadth thick. There is no way it could have been torn.

DEMETRIUS: Exactly. Not by the hand of man anyway.

JACOB: What?

DEMETRIUS: Jacob, it could only have been torn by the hand of God.

LEAH: Jacob, think about it! Only God could have made me well and Demetrius too. God's hand tore the curtain. He saw His Son crucified and He tore the curtain.

JACOB *(deflated, confused):* I saw this Jesus crucified; without the power to save himself from that awful death, or even to defend himself from the insults of those taunting Him at the foot of the cross. He just hung there—completely defenseless. He didn't even open His mouth to refute the scoffers! Why didn't He save himself? Why did He bear all that humiliation and pain?

LEAH: I don't know. I only believe.

DEMETRIUS: That's not all.

JACOB: What?

DEMETRIUS: Some are saying He is risen from the dead. Some have seen the open grave where He lay. He is not there.

JACOB: What do you think, Demetrius?

DEMETRIUS AND LEAH *(together):* He is risen!

JACOB: Take me to the tomb, Demetrius! Let me see for myself! This is too fantastic. I must see where He was. *(Covers his face with his hands.)* If I could only see Him!

DEMETRIUS AND LEAH *(at the same time):* Yes, come with us. We will show you the empty tomb!

LEAH *(grabs Jacob's arm):* Come, let's go now.

(As the three walk toward the door, Hosea rushes in, mutters a greeting, keeps his head down, and heads straight through the curtain to the back room. Demetrius, Leah, and Jacob stop and watch him go to the back.)

HOSEA *(shouts back at them, disappearing behind the curtain):* I don't want to be disturbed, Jacob.

DEMETRIUS *(to Jacob, indicating toward the back room):* He knows.

JACOB: I should stay. We'll have to go later. Please pray for me.

(Cleopas enters.)

CLEOPAS *(glancing around at the sober faces of Demetrius, Leah and Jacob):* Why the downcast looks? "He that hath a bountiful eye shall be blessed; for he giveth of his bread to the poor."[5]

DEMETRIUS: What's that got to do with anything?

CLEOPAS: It means that if you *(waves his hand)*—Oh, never mind. *(Looking toward the back room.)* Is Hosea here?

---

[5] Proverbs 22:9, *KJV*

(Hosea enters holding a quill and some thread.)

HOSEA: Thought I heard you in here, Cleopas. I have wanted to talk with you about—the recent happenings. What think you of this Jesus and His crucifixion?

DEMETRIUS: Yes, what think you, good Cleopas? What think you of the resurrection from the dead and the rending of the Veil to the Most Holy Place?

CLEOPAS *(looking around, then at Hosea):* I've seen the Veil. I can't explain it. And I can't explain the empty tomb either. I've tried, but—

HOSEA: I know. It can't be true that the disciples moved the stone and stole Jesus' body. The tomb was sealed. I saw it. There is no explanation other than the hand of God.

JACOB: Has anybody talked with His disciples?

CLEOPAS *(shaking his head):* We can't find them! They must be hiding out somewhere, afraid that they will meet with the same fate as their Leader if we find them.

JACOB: I heard that the disciple Peter denied he ever knew Jesus.

LEAH: Yes, but he was afraid. You would have been afraid too, Jacob.

JACOB *(offended):* Well, maybe.

CLEOPAS: There is much I just don't understand about this Jesus. He indeed did have the power to heal; that's obvious. At any rate, I will continue to search for answers. *(Hosea nods. Cleopas walks toward the door and looks back.)* Shalom, brothers.

(As he begins to leave through the open doorway, Cleopas stops abruptly, having seen the person of Christ approaching the shop. Cleopas is horrified and backs into the shop, stumbling on his flowing robe as he tries to get out of the way of the person. He hastily tries to correct himself but stumbles farther, still walking backward and staring at Jesus. He drops some coins and ends up sitting on the floor awkwardly, staring into the face of the person he has just seen. Jesus, meanwhile, has entered the store and stands watching Cleopas. Throughout the rest of this scene, all those in the room are staring at Jesus in reverence and fear.)

JESUS: What troubles you, Cleopas? *(Pause.)* Have you nothing to say?

The Weaver's Apprentice

CLEOPAS *(stuttering):* I . . . I, uh—

JESUS: You have found comfort in the quoting of Scripture many times, Cleopas, and with knowledge of the Law you have led many astray. *(Pause as Cleopas is tongue-tied, then continues, slowly.)* Remember King David's prophecy, when he said, "I am poured out like water, and all my bones are out of joint: my heart is like wax; it is melted in the midst of my bowels. My strength is dried up like a potsherd; and my tongue cleaveth to my jaws; and thou hast brought me into the dust of death. For dogs have compassed me: the assembly of the wicked have inclosed me: they pierced my hands and my feet. *(Shows the nail marks in his hands.)* I may tell all my bones: they look and stare upon me. They part my garments among them, and cast lots upon my vesture."[6] It was I who was crucified, Cleopas, and those words foretold my coming. Isaiah said of me, "He was oppressed, and he was afflicted, yet he opened not his mouth: he is brought as a lamb to the slaughter, and as a sheep before her shearers is dumb, so he openeth not his mouth. . . . And he bare the sin of many, and made intercession for the transgressors."[7] You memorized the words with your mind, but your heart did not receive. You became knowledgeable, but gained no wisdom.

CLEOPAS *(swallows, then humbly):* Surely you are the Son of God!

JESUS: I Am.

CLEOPAS: My Lord and my God! I do believe. Forgive me my unbelief.

JESUS: Thou art forgiven. Humble yourself, Cleopas, under the mighty hand of God, that He may exalt you at the proper time. *(Turning to Jacob, who is still staring as if he is frozen in fright.)* Did you not know from the beginning that it was I, Jacob?

JACOB: Well, I thought it was, but—*(Looking at his father.)*

JESUS: Search no more for the ripper of the curtain, Jacob. It was my Father who reached down from Heaven and rent the Veil when the work on the cross was finished. *(Looks at Hosea.)* Not out of anger, Hosea, but to illustrate that the way has been paid for you to enter into His presence. *(Now faces audience, speaking slowly, triumphantly and dramatically, with pauses so the audience can applaud.)* In the past,

---

[6] Psalm 22:14-18, *KJV*
[7] Isaiah 53:7, 12, *KJV*

only a high priest entered the Most Holy Place, and only once a year, and never without blood, which he offered for himself and for the sins of the people.[8] *(Triumphantly, slowly.)* But now I have entered the Most Holy Place once for all by my own blood, having obtained eternal redemption![9] You are made holy by the sacrifice of my body, once for all![10] Therefore, since you can have confidence to enter the Most Holy Place by my blood, by a new and living way opened to you through the curtain, that is, my body, draw near to God with a sincere heart in full assurance of faith.[11] *(The people who are standing now kneel in reverence. Jesus speaks to all those in the room.)* Because you have seen me, you have believed; blessed are those who have not seen and yet have believed.[12]

(Lights fade out and then come back on as Choir sings. All the speaking characters in the play now join those on the stage and face Jesus in worshipful attitudes. Some may bow, some kneel on one knee, some raise their hands in praise and some fold their hands in prayer. Jesus stands with hands outstretched throughout the song, facing the audience.)

CHOIR: "Behold the Lamb" *(or your choice)*

CONGREGATION: "All Hail the Power of Jesus' Name" *(One of the main characters, or the pastor or song director of the church could now direct the congregation to stand and sing. Then close in prayer.)*

---

[8] Hebrews 9:7, *NIV*
[9] Hebrews 9:12, *NIV*
[10] Hebrews 10:10, *NIV*
[11] Hebrews 10:19-22, *NIV*
[12] John 20:29, *NIV*

The Weaver's Apprentice

Mordecai's Testimony

Margaret Cheasebro

Characters:

MORDECAI, who delivers the monologue

The remaining characters do not have speaking parts. They pantomime the action. They sit in the audience, go on stage at the appropriate time, then return to their seats. In a small congregation some people may play more than one character. Those characters are listed together on one line.

JOSEPH OF ARIMATHEA; SIMON PETER; A GUARD; A DISCIPLE

NICODEMUS; JOHN; A GUARD; A DISCIPLE

JESUS

TWO ANGELS

MARY, THE MOTHER OF JAMES AND JOSES

MARY MAGDALENE

SALOME

If others would like parts in the play, let them be disciples who appear in the scene after the resurrection when Jesus shows them his hands, side, and feet.

Props:

A blanket to represent the body of Jesus being carried into the tomb

A tomb with movable rock

A bush. This can be made of cardboard, or more simply, can be a chair draped with a green blanket or green paper.

A chair on which Mordecai can sit

A seal. This can be a wooden plaque placed on the floor or a white piece of butcher paper with a design on it that can be taped to the black paper representing the stone.

A jug of water and a sandwich, both optional

Staging: Staging can be very simple. At stage center create an area to represent the tomb and the stone rolled over the entrance. Do this by placing two large dividers or something similar with a space between them for the tomb entrance. Cover the dividers with brown butcher paper or dark blankets. Using two layers of black butcher paper, cut out a large stone. Attach two black pipe cleaners, using tape and staples, to the upper left and right corners of the stone. Place tacks in three spots at the top of the divider. Wrap the pipe cleaners around tacks one and two so that they support the butcher paper rock over the tomb entrance. When the stone is rolled away, someone from behind the divider can unwrap the pipe cleaners from around the tacks and move the stone over, reattaching them to tacks two and three.

To the left of the tomb, place a bush that can be made from cardboard or brown butcher paper draped over a chair. Beside the bush place the chair on which Mordecai will sit.

MORDECAI: I am Mordecai, keeper of the tombs. People who are superstitious run when they see me coming. I hope you are not superstitious. I'm tired of having people run from me. Do you know what it's like to sit at an outdoor restaurant and have everyone get up and leave as though I had leprosy or something? I'm not contagious—really!

I've seen a lot, though, in my work as a tomb keeper, a lot. I don't talk about it much. But today—today I feel the need to talk. Maybe I'm feeling my age. I don't want this story to go untold. It's a true story and it changed my life.

I've been a keeper of the tombs for more years than I can remember. I've watched people carry their dead into caves carved out of rock or out of a hillside. I've watched them lay the bodies of their loved ones on slabs of rock, bind them up with long lengths of cloth, and cover them with sweet-smelling oils and spices. And I've watched them seal the entrance to the tombs with huge stones they rolled in place and sealed with a wedge to keep in the stench of a decaying body and to keep out animals. I make sure the tombs stay sealed.

People come to mourn the dead. I watch the mourners. They are sad, sometimes tearful, often heartbroken. And why not? Death is final. When you die, that's the end of it. No sense thinking that there may be something beyond death. I know. I've watched over too many tombs. There is finality to death that no one can contest. At least that's what I thought until one Sunday morning not long ago.

I was tending the tombs on a Friday, when Joseph of Arimathea and his friend, Nicodemus, carried the body of a Man named Jesus, who had died on a cross, to a new tomb—a tomb Joseph had planned for his own burial place.

(Joseph of Arimathea and Nicodemus carry a blanket, representing Jesus, into the open tomb. Then they roll a stone in front of it to close the tomb, using the pipe cleaners as described in the staging section.)

MORDECAI: I'd heard about this Man, Jesus. He claimed to be the Son of God. I've never been a religious person. I don't pay much attention to that sort of thing. But this Jesus had a way with people. He drew crowds wherever He went. I saw Him once when He rode into Jerusalem on a little donkey. Something about His eyes and the way He sat as He rode the colt held my attention. I don't know what it was about the Man, but He could hold people's interest, make them drink in every word He said. The religious authorities didn't like Him much. I think they were jealous when the people paid more attention to Him than to them. One thing led to another and they crucified Him.

People always come to me in the end. No one can escape death, not even the famous ones, not even the ones who can draw crowds like Jesus could. Some tombs I watch over more closely than others. Jesus' tomb was one of those. That's because He claimed that if people destroyed His body, or His temple as He called it, He would rise again in three days. So you can believe that I kept a close eye on His tomb. I value my reputation as an expert tomb keeper. You never know what people might do when someone who stirs up so much attention dies. Some of them could get hysterical and try to steal the body. Thrill seekers could try to tamper with the tomb, or a crowd of His friends could sit in front of the tomb, blocking the movement of people who are burying their dead in nearby tombs. You never know what grieving people might try to do. Sometimes their grief makes them a little crazy for a while.

I wasn't the only one worried about what might happen at Jesus' tomb. Pontius Pilate, the Roman procurator of Judea who was in charge of making sure the province ran smoothly, had sentenced Jesus to death on the cross. He was afraid that Jesus' friends would try to make it look like He rose from the dead. So Pilate had the tomb sealed and two guards posted outside.

(Two guards place a seal on the tombstone, then sit outside the tomb.)

MORDECAI: I wasn't satisfied with that. I feel responsible for every tomb in my charge. I report directly to the tomb's owner if anything goes wrong. The guards could report to Pilate, but I was there for Joseph of Arimathea. So I found myself a spot behind some bushes near Jesus' tomb. I brought a sandwich and a jug of water with me and kept watch.

(Mordecai sits in a chair by the bush with a jug of water and a sandwich by his side.)

MORDECAI: For a long time everything was quiet. Then, shortly after midnight on Sunday morning, it felt like the ground was shaking. Then I saw something that made the hair stand straight up on the back of my neck. There was a glow, a bright light that shimmered all around the rock in front of Jesus' tomb. I rubbed my eyes, blinked hard, and hit myself on the head a couple of times to be sure I wasn't seeing things. As I watched, the light glowed brighter and brighter. Then the rock began to roll away, all by itself.

(The person playing the part of Jesus should be behind the divider where the audience cannot see him. He should roll away the stone using the pipe cleaners so the rock appears to be moving by itself.)

MORDECAI: There was no one there—just the light! I was too frightened to move. The guards fell to the ground. Then they jumped up and ran away like scared rabbits.

(Guards fall down, then run away in fear.)

MORDECAI: It's a good thing I stayed to see what happened. Those guards didn't help at all. With the rock rolled back to reveal the tomb entrance, I thought I could make out two figures. They looked like two men, but their garments shone, brilliantly white. Maybe they were angels.

(Two angels enter from stage right and walk into the tomb.)

MORDECAI: They walked into the tomb, and when they came out there were three of them—the two angels and the man named Jesus!

(The two angels and Jesus walk out of the tomb and leave stage right.)

MORDECAI: I was shivering all over with fright. Nothing like this had ever happened before. Death is final—I've always known that. But there was Jesus, and He was talking to the angels as they walked away.

When daybreak came, three women arrived at the tomb. I recognized them from the funeral procession. They were women who were followers of Jesus: Mary Magdalene, Mary the mother of James and Joses, and Salome. They were confused when they saw the stone rolled away from the door. They cautiously entered the tomb.

(The two Marys and Salome enter the tomb, then come out and pantomime wailing.)

MORDECAI: That's when they discovered Jesus was gone. I had to plug my ears to protect them from all the wailing and howling. Those women carried on so. I don't know why women think they have to do that. We all know they're sad. Why do they have to make so much noise? My wife tells me it's their way of expressing their sorrow and letting other people know how much the person was loved. I know she's right. I just wish they wouldn't make so much noise! When the women were so upset, two angels appeared.

(Two angels enter from right and pretend to talk with the women.)

MORDECAI: One of the angels told them Jesus had risen from the dead. He said, "Do not be afraid, for I know that you are looking for Jesus, who was crucified. He is not here; he has risen, just as he said. Come and see the place where he lay. Then go quickly and tell his disciples: 'He has risen from the dead and is going ahead of you into Galilee. There you will see him.' Now I have told you" (Matthew 28:5-7, *NIV*).

(Women pantomime fear and excitement as they and the angels exit stage right.)

MORDECAI: The women were scared, but they also seemed excited, as though they wanted to believe the angels but were too frightened to understand everything they'd been told. All I could do was stay there hidden behind the bushes, trying to figure out how I would explain to Joseph of Arimathea that his tomb had been robbed by angels and that a Man had risen from the dead. He'd believe me like he would a hole in the head. Maybe he'd put a hole in my head.

The women must have spread the word, because pretty soon Simon Peter and John came running to the tomb.

(John enters tomb followed by Simon Peter. They come out mouthing to each other the words, "He's gone.")

MORDECAI: I went to find Joseph of Arimathea myself and tell him what had happened to his tomb. I thought he'd better hear it from me first. His reaction surprised me. I thought he would be very upset, but after he stared at me in disbelief for a second, he began shouting, "Praise the Lord! Jesus really *is* the Son of God. He rose from the dead. Don't you see, Mordecai? He rose from the dead!"

What a nut case, I told myself. But in the days that followed, I heard a lot of stories about Jesus appearing to Mary Magdalene, walking with two of His followers on the road to Emmaus and even entering a locked room to show His disciples the wounds in His hands, feet, and side from His crucifixion experience.

Pilate and the Jewish leaders tried to cover up what happened. They tried to say the disciples stole His body. But I was there. I know it didn't happen that way. I know what I saw. Death is not always final. Jesus did rise from the dead. He did what He said He would do. Three days after He died, He rose again.

Joseph of Arimathea, Nicodemus, and I have become friends since then. I too have become a follower of Jesus Christ. This Man who could attract crowds but only attracted my curiosity while He lived has, in His death and resurrection, captured my heart. Joseph, Nicodemus, and I sometimes talk about the miraculous occurrence on that Sunday morning. And we all believe. No, we don't believe, we know. We know without a doubt that Jesus rose from the dead. We know He is who He claimed to be, the Son of God.

I am still a keeper of the tombs. I have never seen any other person rise from the dead. But I will never doubt what I saw. No matter what the Jewish leaders try to say, Jesus really did rise from the dead. And that knowledge gives me hope. There is life beyond death. Jesus came to tell us that. He had a message of love and forgiveness, a message of hope and healing. And I am a happier person because of it. I know now that Jesus truly is the Son of God and that He lives, even though He once died. He lives in you and He lives in me. Glory be to His name!

(People in the audience who have appeared in the monologue stand up and say, with Mordecai, in a loud voice, "Hallelujah! Christ is risen. Hallelujah! Praise the Lord!")

In the Shadow of the Cross

Lillian Robbins

Characters:
JASON, Father
TIMMY, Son
ANNA, Mother
JESUS
SIMON
SOLDIER
MARY MAGDALENE
MARY, THE MOTHER OF JAMES
SALOME
ANGEL
EXTRA PEOPLE

Scene I—Outside Jason's house
Scene II—Roadway to Calvary
Scene III—Area near the tomb on the day after the Sabbath

Costumes: Bible-time clothes, angel's attire

Props: Stool, whittling knife, wood, basket, items for basket, cross, bushes, bags of spices, floodlight

Scene I

Outside Jason's house, Jason is sitting on a stool, whittling. In a way, he is singing no special tune of a song but the following words.

JASON: O, God Almighty, the Creator of all nature, look down upon Thy children and—

TIMMY *(carrying a basket, rushes in):* Father, Father, something terrible has happened. I heard it at the market.

JASON: What is it, Timmy? What terrible thing has happened?

TIMMY: They went there and took Him, Jesus, last night. He was in the Garden of Gethsemane.

JASON: Calm down a little, Timmy. Now tell me, who went there?

TIMMY: A big crowd of people, the chief priests and elders and a lot of other people they had with them. They went to arrest Jesus.

JASON: To arrest Jesus? Why? And why would they go to the garden at night?

TIMMY: The women at the market said that one of His apostles was a traitor. That apostle told the enemies of Jesus where to find Him.

JASON: One of His apostles a traitor? I wonder who it could be. Was it Philip? Or Bathlolomew? Or Peter?

TIMMY: I don't think so. Those names don't sound like what the women said.

JASON: Well now, there are twelve of them, you know.

TIMMY: I know, Father. I've seen them with Jesus. But I don't know all their names.

JASON: Maybe it was Andrew.

TIMMY: No, I remember him. You know when Jesus fed all of us that day where He was preaching. You remember, we had gone there to visit Nathan, and we went with him to see Jesus. Andrew found my friend that day, the one who had the bread and fishes.

JASON: I remember. We all ate and there was a lot of food left. Let's see, then, one of the apostles is James.

TIMMY: I don't think that was the one. The men I heard talking said something about the apostle who always carried the bag of money. Something about him wanting to get some money of his own.

JASON: Then that would have been Judas Iscariot.

TIMMY: That's it! That's the name they said.

JASON: Oh, how terrible, one of His own apostles. How could he turn Jesus over to His enemies?

TIMMY: It must have been for the money.

JASON: I know many of the Pharisees and elders have been trying to get something to accuse Jesus of. They have wanted to get rid of Him. But they couldn't find anything wrong with Him. He has done only good for people all His life.

TIMMY: If they have heard Him teach or seen Him heal people, they should know that.

JASON: Some folks say nothing good can come out of Nazareth. Don't they know that God can create that which is good anywhere?

TIMMY: I believed Jesus. I believe everything He said is true.

JASON: Tell me, Son, just what all did you hear at the market? I wonder why Jesus was in the garden at night.

TIMMY: I heard before this happened that sometimes Jesus would go there to pray to God.

JASON: People crowded around Him so much, I suppose that was a place He could be alone.

TIMMY: But He was not alone. Some of His apostles were with Him. The women thought all of the apostles were there. Of course, Judas came late to lead the priests and elders to where Jesus was.

JASON: If it was so dark at night, it is a wonder they had not mistakenly arrested the wrong man.

TIMMY: No, they had an agreement with Judas. Judas would kiss Jesus, and then His enemies would know which one He was.

JASON: I wonder if there was any resistance. I remember something Jesus taught about turning the other cheek. I wonder what He did when they came to take Him away.

TIMMY: He didn't resist, but one of His apostles did. He drew his sword and struck one of the servants of the priest. It actually cut off the man's ear.

JASON: I might say that served him right, but that is not the attitude Jesus teaches.

TIMMY: You know what Jesus did? He told the apostle to put away his sword. Then He picked up the servant's ear and put it back in place right on the side of his head.

JASON: What a Master! What a heart of compassion! There has never been anyone like Him before.

ANNA *(entering):* Timmy, did you get everything I asked for?

TIMMY: I hope so, Mother. I was so excited, I'm not sure.

ANNA: What was there to be excited about?

JASON: It's what he heard at the market, Anna. Jesus' enemies have arrested Him.

ANNA: What for? He is a good man.

JASON: We will tell you all about it later. Is the meal ready?

In the Shadow of the Cross

ANNA: Yes, I was just coming to tell you. I didn't realize it would take Timmy so long to get back from the market, but I had enough food in the cupboard to prepare this meal anyway.

JASON: Then we will go in to eat and after that we'll tell you the news.

(All exit.)

Scene II

People are gathered beside the roadway to Calvary. Jason, Anna, and Timmy enter.

JASON: Anna, Timmy, be sure to stay close to me. It appears as though many people are expecting Jesus to come this way. Just look at all the people. They keep on coming from everywhere.

ANNA: I want to be here, but I don't know if I can bear to see Him going to Calvary.

JASON: I know, Anna, but you insisted on coming along. You know, to begin with, just Timmy and I were coming alone.

TIMMY: It will be all right, Mother. You know this is our last chance to get a look at Jesus.

ANNA: I don't know if you are going to be able to see, Timmy. There are so many people, and you are so short.

JASON: I'll try to make a way for him.

ANNA: I wonder how all of this happened. How could Pilate condemn Jesus to death? Jesus had done nothing wrong.

JASON: To begin with, the elders and priests and captains of the temple arrested Jesus. They took Him before the high priest and the Sanhedrin. Of course, they didn't really have evidence against Him but when false witnesses are paid to deceive the court, the innocent can be found guilty. It was all just a mock trial.

TIMMY: I heard that Pilate didn't really find Jesus guilty.

JASON: No, he didn't. He even washed his hands in a pan of water to try to clear himself of any responsibility in condemning Jesus to die.

ANNA: Then why did he do it?

JASON: The Pharisees had stirred up a mob of people who were there crying out, "Crucify Him, crucify Him!"

ANNA: But I thought they always let one prisoner go free.

JASON: The mob wanted to free Barabbas, not Jesus.

ANNA: But Barabbas is a criminal.

JASON: Pilate didn't want to have the people turn against him. His job is always at stake.

TIMMY: If I could have been there, I would have screamed louder than anybody, "Let Jesus go! Let Jesus go!"

SOLDIER *(loud voice offstage):* Go on there. Don't stop every few steps. *(Silence.)* Go on, I told you. It's a long way up that hill. *(Sound of cross dragging on road.)* Are you such a weakling? Can't you even carry a cross on your shoulders? Move it, I tell you. Move it on.

ANNA: Oh, how dreadful!

TIMMY: Why doesn't somebody help Him?

JASON: Make way. He's coming.

(Jesus and Simon wind through the crowd from front toward back of stage.)

TIMMY: It's too heavy. That great big wooden cross is too heavy for Him to carry.

ANNA: He's too weak. They have almost beaten the life out of Him already. Don't they know that He is too weak?

(Just a few steps onto the stage and Jesus falls.)

SOLDIER: You, over there. Come and lift this cross.

(No one comes forward.)

SOLDIER *(takes arm of Simon):* You there, take that cross. We've got to get it up that hill. The other two crosses are there already.

(Simon takes cross and moves on.)

SOLDIER *(takes arm of Jesus):* Come on, you. This is your last walk, you know.

ANNA *(and others are weeping softly):* Jason, can't we do something?

JASON: There is nothing we can do, Anna. It's in the power of the law.

TIMMY: But God's power is stronger than the law. So why is this happening?

JASON: We don't understand it now, Son, but we will someday.

(People follow Jesus offstage on far side.)

JASON *(taking Anna's arm):* We had better go home, Anna.

ANNA: Let's go a little farther, Jason. They will soon be at the top of the hill. *(Pause.)* I can't see what they are doing. They are out of sight.

JASON: Then we may as well go home now. *(Turns to leave.)*

TIMMY: Wait, Father. Wait just a minute.

JASON: Why, Timmy? We can't see any more now.

TIMMY: I know. But I just can't go yet.

(Sound of nails being driven in Jesus' hands and feet.)

ANNA: Oh, no! That awful sound!

JASON: They nail His hands and feet to the cross. That sound means they are about ready to lift Him up and drop the cross in the hole in the ground.

(Thud sound.)

TIMMY: Now they have dropped the cross into the ground.

JASON: "And I, if I be lifted up from the earth, will draw all men unto me" (John 12:32, *KJV*). Jesus said that one time. Now He has been lifted up. *(Turning to Anna.)* Come on Anna, Timmy. Jesus will hang there for hours until He dies. I suppose His close friends are there at the cross, but there is nothing we can do.

ANNA: If only God would have protected Him and let Him continue His work. His teaching was so wonderful. And He could heal any sickness. He could do everything.

JASON: We don't understand, but God has a purpose. We must trust the Lord. *(All leave.)*

Scene III

Area near tomb on the first day after the Sabbath. Jason, Anna, and Timmy enter.

JASON: Wait, we better stop here. *(Stops behind the bush.)*

TIMMY: Why, Father? We are not there yet.

JASON: I know.

ANNA: They buried Jesus in a tomb owned by Joseph of Arimathea.

JASON: I know, but we just better stop here.

ANNA: Can't we go to the tomb?

JASON: No, we will stop right here. The tomb is just up that way, but we better not go any farther.

TIMMY: Papa, do you think we would be in danger if we went to the tomb?

JASON: That is really not the problem, Son. I don't know why, but I just know that we must stop here.

ANNA: Someone is coming this way.

(Jason, Anna, and Timmy step back to be partially hidden by the bush. Mary, Mary Magdalene, and Salome enter.)

MARY: I still don't understand it all. I know we are going to the tomb where Jesus was buried, but why is all of this happening?

MARY MAGDALENE: You know, Mary, we didn't have an opportunity to take the spices for His body because the Sabbath was coming immediately after Joseph of Arimathea took Jesus' body from the cross.

SALOME: Now the Sabbath is over, we can take spices to the tomb.

MARY: I know why we are going to the tomb now. What I don't understand is why God let them kill Jesus.

SALOME: There are many things we don't understand, Mary. But we do know that Jesus was from God. There must be a good reason He had to die.

MARY MAGDALENE: How will we be able to get inside the tomb to put our spices on the body of Jesus? That big stone blocks the entrance to the grave.

MARY: And of course we can't move it. All three of us together are not strong enough.

SALOME: I know you are right. But all I know is that I just felt that I had to go there this morning. The Sabbath is over and now we must complete the traditional burial arrangements.

MARY MAGDALENE: But how can we do that if we can't even move that stone?

(Sound of an earthquake.)

MARY: Something is happening off that way, out where the tomb is.

(A bright light appears ahead. The women huddle together.)

ANGEL: Don't be afraid. I know that you have come here to seek the body of Jesus. But He is not here. He is risen from the grave. *(Pause.)* You are amazed. I can see that. But come, the stone is moved away from the door of the cave. You can go right in and see where the body of Jesus lay. Then you will truly realize that He is not here. He is alive again.

(The angel and women exit.)

MARY *(offstage in loud voice):* He is risen! He's alive!

ANGEL: Yes, He is alive. Now go and tell His disciples, and of course tell Peter. They must go to Galilee. They will see Jesus there.

(The women rush back on stage and exit the other side.)

ANNA: Jason, Timmy, did you hear that? Jesus came forth out of the tomb. He's alive!

TIMMY: Jesus is alive! *(Dances around repeating.)* Jesus is alive! Jesus is alive! Hallelujah! Jesus is alive!

JASON: Praise the Lord God! He freed Jesus from the bonds of death. Jesus is alive. We may see Him again.

TIMMY: I want to go to Galilee. I want to see Jesus.

JASON: That message you heard the angel tell the women was just for the apostles. We'll just have to wait and see what happens.

ANNA: Hurry, let's go home. I want to tell all my friends.

TIMMY *(as they leave):* Hallelujah! Jesus is alive!

I Am There

Lillian Robbins

Share with me as I pretend that I am a young person living in Jerusalem during the days of Jesus.

There is excitement in Jerusalem. It is time for the Passover. Just a few days ago, a Man came into the city riding on a donkey. Crowds of people laid garments in His path or gathered palm branches to spread along the way. That Man I have heard so much about, Jesus of Nazareth, He has come.

Every time I hear about how He made the blind to see or the deaf to hear, I am thrilled right to the bone. Maybe now that He is in Jerusalem, I'll get to see Him.

Tonight I'm going to take a walk out to the Mount of Olives. I have heard that Jesus goes there sometimes.

What is that I see way on down the path? Over there underneath that big olive tree? Looks like someone kneeling by a stump. I'll just creep in closer.

It must be Jesus. I can hear words, "My Father, if it is possible, may this cup be taken from me. Yet not as I will, but as you will." He is in agony. It looks like blood is streaming out of the pores of His skin. Now He is lying full out on His face, but He keeps right on talking to God. And what is that beside Him, an angel?

I can't follow as Jesus moves away. But there are men coming into the garden carrying torches. They have swords. One man goes up to Jesus and kisses Him on the cheek. The others gather around and take Jesus like a prisoner. Jesus' friends are running away. I guess they are afraid, but don't they know that Jesus has power? He could get away from those men if He wanted to. Maybe I better go on home.

I didn't sleep much last night. I kept thinking about what I saw. And a most unusual thing happened after that. I heard a rooster crow during the night. I'm going out again and see if I can find out what happened to Jesus.

There is a crowd of people along that way over there. Maybe I can get close enough to see. It's Jesus! He looks so tired, so weak. And no wonder, He is carrying a cross on His shoulders up that hill. Oh, no!

He has fallen to the ground. There, another man picks up the cross to carry it, but Jesus trudges on.

At the top of the hill, they lay Jesus on that cross. The sound of the hammer driving spikes into His hands and feet makes me feel sick. And that loud thud as the cross hits the bottom of that hole is almost deafening. I just can't bear it—Jesus, who is perfect, to be treated like a criminal. Jesus is going to die right there beside those thieves.

The Sabbath has passed. The women said that Joseph of Arimathea took the body of Jesus and buried him. I'll just go there and see. The dawn is just breaking, but I'm not afraid. It would be a beautiful day if it were not for all the sorrow in my heart.

Up ahead I see some women walking along and talking about that huge stone that was rolled to the mouth of the cave where Jesus is buried. They want to put spices on the body, but they are not strong enough to roll that stone away.

What a bright light up ahead! I've never seen anything like it before. I can see the grave site now, and the stone has been rolled away from the tomb. There is someone there, sitting on the stone. But that's not just a person. His long, white robe is as white as snow, and he gleams like lightning. He must be an angel.

The women are afraid, but the angel is talking to them. "He is not here; he has risen. Come and see the place where he lay."

Jesus is risen! He is not dead! He has won victory over death! I can go home now. Everything is all right.

But who is that over there talking to one of the women? She is telling Him she is sad because she can't find the body of Jesus.

The Man turns to her and says, "Mary."

She exclaims, "Master!" Now she knows this is Jesus, risen from the dead. Jesus, alive forevermore.

We didn't live then as that young girl may have, but today we have the same exuberant spirit as we proclaim, "Jesus is alive! He has conquered sin and death and reigns in Heaven where He is preparing a place for us."

I'm Glad It Wasn't Me

Paula Reed

Good Friday Service

OPENING PRAYER

*(**Note to the Director:** The following is a very graphic, detailed description of a crucifixion. It is provided for the director's information. Because it is of a sensitive nature, please use what is appropriate for your audience. You may use all of it, some of it, or none of it. The point is to emphasize the degree of Jesus' suffering.)*

READER: What is crucifixion? A medical doctor provides a physical description: The cross is placed on the ground and the exhausted man is quickly thrown backward with his shoulders pressed against the wood. The legionnaire drives a heavy, square wrought-iron nail through the wrist deep into the wood. Quickly he moves to the other side and repeats the action, being careful not to pull the arms too tightly. The cross is then lifted into place. The left foot is pressed backward against the right foot, and with both feet extended, toes down, a nail is driven through the arch of each, leaving the knees flexed. The victim is now crucified. As he slowly sags down with more weight on the nails in the wrists, excruciating fiery pain shoots along the fingers and up the arms to explode in the brain—the nails in the wrists are putting pressure on the median nerves. As he pushes himself upward to avoid this stretching torment, he places the full weight on the nails through his feet. Again he feels the searing agony of the nails tearing through the nerves between the bones of his feet. As the arms tire, cramps sweep through his muscles, knotting them in deep, relentless, throbbing pain. With these cramps comes the inability to push upward to breathe. Air can be drawn into the lungs but not exhaled. He fights to raise himself in order to get even one small breath. Finally, carbon dioxide builds up in the lungs and in the bloodstream, and the cramps partially subside. Spasmodically, he is able to push himself upward to exhale and bring in life-giving oxygen. There are hours of limitless pain, cycles of twisting, joint-wrenching cramps, intermittent partial asphyxiation, searing pain as

I'm Glad It Wasn't Me

tissue is torn from his lacerated back as he moves up and down against rough timber. Then another agony begins: a deep, crushing pain deep in the chest as the pericardium slowly fills with serum and begins to compress the heart. It is now almost over—the loss of tissue fluids has reached a critical level—the compressed heart is struggling to pump heavy, thick, sluggish blood into the tissues—the tortured lungs are making frantic effort to gasp in small gulps of air. He can feel the chill of death creeping through his tissues. Finally, he can allow his body to die. All this the Bible records with the simple words: "And they crucified him" (Mark 15:24, *NIV*).

Six people are seated around a table to partake of Communion. Each person is frozen until it is his turn to speak. Person dressed as Jesus enters holding loaf and cup. As he approaches stage he stops and says, "I tell you the truth, one of you will betray me" (Matthew 26:21, NIV). Moves behind group and says, "Take and eat; this is my body given for you; do this in remembrance of me"(Matthew 26:26 and Luke 22:19, NIV), then places loaf on table. Then he says, "Drink from it, all of you. This is my blood of the covenant, which is poured out for many for the forgiveness of sins" (Matthew 26:27, 28, NIV), then places cup on table. Remains standing behind group and places each person's sign on cross after each speaks. Sound of hammer and nail is heard offstage as he does this.

PERSON 1: I can't imagine how I'd feel if Jesus had told me I would betray Him. But I wasn't there, and it couldn't have been me anyway. I've been a Christian practically my whole life! Raised in the church, attended hundreds of Sunday school classes, listened to countless sermons. No, not me—I wouldn't betray Jesus. I've led a clean life—a good life. Not like some other people I know who think they're good but they're really not. Oh, I'm not saying I'm perfect, but at least I haven't murdered anyone or stolen from anyone. Sure, I've probably told a lie or two or even had some impure thoughts along the way, but nothing major. No, I can't even imagine what it must have been like to be Judas. I'm just glad it wasn't me who sent You to the cross. *(Partakes of Communion as* *sound of hammer and nail is heard in background and sign "PRIDE" is placed on the cross. Then freezes.)*

PERSON 2: I will never understand how Jesus could have called Judas His friend, knowing full well what he was going to do. Jesus even washed the feet of that betrayer—how could He do that? I mean, I know what it's like to be betrayed by a Christian brother. To have someone call you "friend" to your face but "foe" behind your back. *(Shakes head.)* It was a big mistake to go into business with Joe. I lost everything—my house—my job—my savings—all because of him. I offered him my trust and he repaid me with betrayal. I never want to see that man again as long as I live and I long for the day he will get what's due him. No, I could never wash Joe's feet and the last thing I would call him is "friend." I'm just glad the sin of betrayal is on his shoulders—not mine. *(Partakes of Communion as sound of hammer and nail is heard in background and sign "HATRED" is placed on the cross. Then freezes.)*

PERSON 3: I'm sure this Communion time is hard for many people here tonight. Why, next to me there's poor Mr. Brown who lost so much due to his business partner, Joe—and Joe was even a deacon in our church! What a scandal that was! I was just telling someone the other day that it's no wonder the poor man is consumed with hatred. I probably would be too. At least Joe has the decency not to show his face around here anymore, unlike some other people I know. I can't believe *she's* here tonight. Just wait until I get home and call Dorothy and tell her that the she-devil who lured her husband into an affair is actually here at church! She's probably just trying to catch another poor, unsuspecting man. Who does she think she is anyway? But she's not the only one. I've seen at least a dozen people here tonight who I know have stories that would curl your hair. And, Lord, You know we've discussed these prayer concerns in our ladies prayer group time and time again. But the list just keeps growing. *(Sighs, pauses.)* Well, I for one am glad that I don't have the weight of their sins around *my* neck. *(Partakes of Communion as sound of hammer and nail is heard in background and sign "GOSSIP" is placed on the cross. Then freezes.)*

I'm Glad It Wasn't Me

PERSON 4: I have to admit something, Lord. These Good Friday Services really get me down. They're just so serious and depressing. I know that You endured terrible suffering, but why should I walk away from here feeling so guilty? I mean, it's not like I was even there—I'm not the one who sold You out for thirty pieces of silver. I could never do that. *(Pauses, looks at watch.)* I wonder how long this is going to last tonight. I work hard all week and weekends are my only time to kick back and relax. I can hardly wait to get home, turn on the TV, and watch some ESPN. Then, of course, the rest of the weekend we're going to the lake with friends and try out that shiny new boat I bought. Boy, what a beauty she is too. I've got plans for her all summer long. Lord, You understand that weekends are meant for lots of "R and R," don't You? After all, You're the one who declared we should rest on the Sabbath. And I agree! Besides, I'll be back in church regularly again by September. We'll get together then, I promise. *(Partakes of Communion as sound of hammer and nail is heard in background and sign "IDOLATRY" is placed on the cross. Then freezes.)*

PERSON 5: I'm really trying hard to stay focused here tonight. It would have been helpful if my wife hadn't got me all out of sorts right before we came to church. I can't believe she got so upset over those magazines she found in my desk. "Dirty" she called them— "disgusting" she said. They're just pictures—it's not like I'm going to *do* anything. I'm not exactly betraying her by just thinking about some of those beautiful women. Besides, I've always been told that I could "look, but don't touch," and I haven't touched anyone but my wife since we've been married. That ought to mean something to her. Well, it's a good thing she didn't check my computer. She'd really be mad about that. *(Pauses.)* But I can't worry about that right now. I should be focused on You, Lord. After all, this is the night we remember how You were betrayed by one of Your followers. I'm just glad it wasn't me. *(Partakes of Communion as sound of hammer and nail is heard in background and sign "IMPURE THOUGHTS" is placed on the cross. Then freezes.)*

PERSON 6: This time of the year I always reflect on what it took for a man like Judas to betray You, Lord. He walked with You, listened to

You, prayed with You, and yet, he sought to destroy You. The hunger for power and an earthly kingdom must have done him in. I could never forgive myself either if I'd been the one who sent You to the cross. *(Pauses, short laugh.)* But my husband says I'm going to send *him* to an early grave if I don't stop overspending. Well, it's not as if I *try* to do that. It's not my fault that our children want certain clothes and those clothes are so expensive. We can't have them ridiculed at school, You know. And I'm not the only one who wanted our beautiful new house. It is unfortunate that it was beyond our budget. Besides, if my husband would just push himself a little harder he could get that promotion that would help us handle the lifestyle we enjoy. *(Pause.)* Sorry, Lord, I got a little off track with my meditation here. I know it must have hurt terribly to have one of Your very own betray You for money. I'm just glad it wasn't me. *(Partakes of Communion as sound of hammer and nail is heard in background and sign "GREED" is placed on the cross. Then freezes.)*

SONG: "Does He Still Feel the Nails?"

NARRATOR: "God made him who had no sin to be sin for us, so that in him we might become the righteousness of God" (2 Corinthians 5:21, *NIV*). It was all of us, wasn't it? We would like to think that we aren't guilty of spilling God's own blood or of nailing His precious hands and feet to the cross—but we are. The Bible says in Romans 3:23 *(NIV)*, "For all have sinned and fall short of the glory of God." All of us have, without exception. But Christ paid the ransom once for all in that He took all our sins and nailed them to the cross. All of our sins gone, without exception. His innocence took on our guilt, His death became our redemption. He paid it all so that we could have it all. Yet if we claim Christ as our Savior, but continue to allow sin to have a stranglehold on our lives, then we have emptied the cross of its power over sin. And if we continue to feel the defeat of sin over us, then we deny Christ's victory over sin. You see, if the cross of Christ is really the cross of our lives, then we need to take that struggle to the cross and leave it there. No denial, no pretending, just honesty. First John 1:9 *(NIV)* says, "If we confess our sins, he is faithful and just and will forgive us our

I'm Glad It Wasn't Me

sins and purify us from all unrighteousness." Tonight we're going to do something a little different as we focus on the cross. Is there an area of your life that you have not completely given to Christ? Some dark, little corner of your heart that continues to raise its ugly head and threaten your relationship to Christ? If so, I urge you to write that down on the paper provided and make your way to the cross and leave it there. No one will look at it. It will be a symbolic act between you and Christ, that you accept His promise of forgiveness and His victory over your sin. Would all of you join me as our heads are bowed and as we meditate on the power of the cross and consider prayerfully, each in our own way, what we need to leave at the foot of the cross?

SONG

COMMUNION MEDITATION: If it were our choice, would we have written the story of redemption the way God did? With followers who would flee and disciples who would deny? Would we have endured suffering and agony when we were innocent for those who were not? I doubt if we would, but God did. We would ask, "But isn't there a way that would be less painful?" and God would reply, "But it wouldn't be love." Romans 5:8 *(NIV)* says, "But God demonstrates his own love for us in this: While we were still sinners, Christ died for us." The truth is, Jesus would rather go to the cross for us than go to Heaven without us. We did nothing to deserve it and we can add nothing to it. Jesus wore a crown of thorns because He had a father's heart and He loves each one of us as if there were only one of us to love. Let's gather around His table, giving thanks to God for His matchless, unfailing love demonstrated to us through the cross.

COMMUNION SONG

COMMUNION

CLOSING REMARKS AND PRAYER

He Is Not Here!
The Promise from the Tomb
Paula Reed

Characters: MARY MAGDALENE, PETER, AND JOHN

Props: For this sunrise service you need a huge open tomb, big enough to see the strips of cloth lying on the slab inside. Stone should be rolled to one side. Use greenery and rocks to convey outdoor setting. Scriptures are from the *New International Version*.

Each character comes forward, one at a time, and speaks directly to the audience.

MARY *(appears at the tomb, lost in her own thoughts, sees the audience and appears somewhat startled, then begins talking):* Oh! I guess I shouldn't be surprised seeing you here. Several of us have already gathered here earlier this morning to witness this amazing event. My name is Mary Magdalene and I, along with two other women, came here earlier to anoint the body of Jesus with perfumes and spices. It was to be my final act of service to my Lord. You can't begin to imagine my confusion when I discovered the tomb was empty! Empty! How my heart was broken. Why would someone take His body? To find Him gone was almost more than I could bear. These past three days have been the longest, the darkest days of my life, three days of total anguish and desperation.

Do any of you know what it's like to watch, helplessly, as all of your hopes and dreams for your future vanish before your very eyes? You see, before I knew Jesus I had no hopes and dreams—no future. My life was enslaved to the torments of demons—demons that were destroying my life, and I was looked upon with disgust and pity. Whenever I did have a rational thought, it was only that I wished I could die. But then came the glorious day I met Jesus of Nazareth and I became a living miracle! He looked upon me, not with disgust and pity, but with compassion. Then He touched me and my life was never the same. He stilled my trembling hands and quieted my raging heart. Tenderly, graciously, He healed me and gave me life!

So thankful was I that I would have followed Him anywhere—and I did! I followed Him from village to village as He explained the Scriptures, as He healed the sick and afflicted, as He loved and cared for all people. I followed Him all the way to the cross where I watched my Lord suffer at the hands of Roman cruelty; where I watched Him, bruised and bleeding, hanging on that rough, wooden cross. I still don't quite understand it. And you might think it strange that I, as a woman, would stay and watch His crucifixion. But how could I abandon Him after all He'd done for me? How could I abandon the very one who healed with such compassion and taught with such authority—whose very life was an example of love? I'm ashamed to say I found myself wishing once again my life was over when I heard Him say from the cross, "It is finished." Darkness fell not only over the earth, but through my very heart and soul as well. And as I walked the path to this tomb this morning I was heavy of heart and barren of hope. But as I told you, when we got here, the tomb was empty! An angel said to us, "He is not here. Go now and tell the good news." So I ran. I ran to the disciples and said, "They have taken the Lord out of the tomb. He has risen and is going into Galilee!" *(Mary sits off to one side of the tomb as Peter enters.)*

PETER: It is good to see that the news is already spreading. I'm sure that you've come here to see for yourselves if the tomb is indeed empty. I tell you the truth—He is not here! I am Peter, one of Jesus' disciples, the "rock" as Jesus used to call me, and I too have come to see. I really can't describe to you my feelings as I ran to the tomb. I wondered where His body was and why someone would do this to Jesus and to those of us who followed Him. I was puzzled, confused, and even angry! Couldn't we be allowed to grieve and mourn in peace? To have His grave disturbed was unthinkable! And as I ran I was ready to fight the Roman centurions guarding His tomb if necessary and make them tell me what they had done with Jesus. Probably wasn't one of the best ideas I'd had. They would have killed me before I even drew my sword. Jesus always said I was a little too impulsive. I have this problem of speaking before thinking—of reacting to the moment instead of allowing the moment to pass.

There was the time I tried to walk on the water. The disciples and I were out on the boat when a strong wind came up. A figure appeared on the lake, walking toward us *on the water*! I tell you, we were shaken. But then we heard Him call, "Take courage! It is I. Don't be afraid." (Matthew 14:27). My heart danced with joy at the words of Jesus, our Teacher, and all I wanted to do was jump out of the boat and go to Him. And I did, or I tried to. I was walking, just like Jesus, on the water; but I became frightened at the wind and the waves that surrounded me. I looked away from Him and began to sink. I cried out to Jesus, "Lord, save me!" and He did. Oh, if only I had not taken my eyes off Jesus. Do you know what it's like to be looking right at Jesus and then something causes you to turn away and your faith begins to falter? I wanted to prove myself to Jesus, but instead, once again, He proved himself to me. He always held on to me—through all my questions, through all my doubts, my fears. He held on to me and never let go. But I did. I'm the one who slipped from His grasp.

Just a few days ago, Jesus told us that He must leave and that we could not follow. He said, "You will all fall away on account of me, for it is written: 'I will strike the shepherd, and the sheep of the flock will be scattered'" (Matthew 26:31). And I said to Him, "Even if all fall away on account of you, I never will" (Matthew 26:33). I meant it, I really did. But when Jesus needed me most, I denied Him. Not once, but three times—just as He said I would. I left Him, alone, to suffer at the hands of religious hypocrisy while I hid in fear. You have no idea the depth of remorse I felt for denying my Lord Jesus, and this after I had declared Him to be the Christ, the Son of the living God! When I realized what I had done, I wept bitter tears, but by then it was too late. Jesus had been taken to be crucified. There He died, alone, on the cruel, rugged cross. It should have been me. I was the one deserving death! He did nothing wrong, but He was the one who took the nails. So you see, when Mary told John and I that the tomb was empty, I wanted so much to believe. And so we ran as if our very lives depended on it. *(Peter remains off to one side of the tomb as John enters.)*

JOHN: When Mary came to us and told us the news, I thought she had lost her mind. I could not understand how the tomb could be empty

He Is Not Here! The Promise from the Tomb

and yet I could not get here fast enough to see for myself. And I see we are not alone—that you also have come to see. I'm the disciple known as John, and when I got to the tomb, I looked but did not go in. I just wasn't ready to see Jesus like that—lifeless, without breath and spirit.

You see, Jesus was more than my teacher, He was my close friend. I would sit in awe at His teachings but I was even more amazed that He loved me like a brother. He loved me for who I really am, not who I sometimes pretended to be. That, my friends, is a powerful love. That kind of love motivates you to action, although sometimes my actions were a little misguided. There was the time my brother, James, and I wanted to call down fire from Heaven on a village that refused to welcome Jesus. Surely they were deserving of that! But Jesus said, no, that He didn't come to destroy lives, but to save them. From then on He called us Sons of Thunder. You know, when I think about it, I have a hard time understanding why Jesus wanted any of us for His disciples. Sometimes we are temperamental, impulsive, slow to understand, of little faith, and even selfish. Next to Jesus, we are a sorry lot. We would even argue among ourselves about who would be the greatest, and once I even went so far as to ask if I could have a special place in His kingdom. I really messed up on that one. But Jesus took us all in, with all our weaknesses, all our failings, and made us His disciples. He commanded us to love one another by first showing us *how* to love by His example. I tell you the truth, that even as He hung on the cross He asked His Father in Heaven to forgive the very ones who had beaten and tortured Him then drove the nails through His hands and feet. "Forgive them," He said! Even in death, His life was an example of love. And this morning, as I looked in the tomb, all the emotions of the past few days came pouring over me and I had to step back. Then Peter rushed in, and as he came out he had a look of complete amazement on his face. I then went in and saw for myself the cause for such amazement. Jesus' body had not been unwrapped and stolen—the grave clothes lay there completely undisturbed. His body had passed right through the trappings of death! I still don't fully understand it. But I saw it and believed. And so I say to you, He is not here!

SONG: *(Use a song of your choice.)*

(All three leave during the song. At the end of the song, all three return to center stage together.)

MARY: I understand why they didn't believe me at first—it did seem incredible. But at least they came to see, as you did. When Peter and John left, I stayed behind and was so overwhelmed I began to cry. I didn't know there were any tears left. I started to turn away and it was then that I saw Him! Oh, I didn't know it at first. I even thought He was the gardener. But then He spoke my name and I knew. A more beautiful sound I've never heard than that of my Lord's voice calling to me. You see, I never expected to actually *see* Him, but I was overjoyed when I did. I didn't meet the risen Lord until I discovered the empty tomb. What if I'd stayed away? I could have just missed the promise from the tomb. I tell you the truth. He is risen! He is risen indeed!

PETER: I ran right into the tomb because I couldn't wait to see if it was true. Was He really gone? And after I saw, I remembered the words of Jesus. He had said, "I am going away and I am coming back to you. . . . I have told you now before it happens, so . . . you will believe" (John 14:28, 29). But I had been so filled with grief and guilt that I was blinded to the truth. But now I know and the truth has set me free! He is not here—that's His promise from the tomb. And I declare to you that Jesus of Nazareth has been raised from the dead because it was impossible for death to keep its hold on Him! He is risen—He is risen indeed!

JOHN: We were as close as anyone to the teachings of Jesus and yet our fears, our weakened faith, kept us from believing. We saw defeat instead of victory. But Jesus was victorious! And because He lives, we can live! Jesus said, "For God so loved the world that he gave his one and only Son, that whoever believes in him shall not perish but have eternal life" (John 3:16). This life is real and we are all witnesses of that life. Look and see for yourselves that He is risen! He is risen indeed!

MARY: He is the King of kings.
JOHN: And Lord of lords!

He Is Not Here! The Promise from the Tomb

PETER: He is the Christ, the Son of the Living God!
SONG: "King of Kings" *(by Sandi Patti)*

(Someone portraying Jesus could step out of the tomb halfway through this song as light illuminates him from behind with the three characters bowed on the ground before him. A second version would be to have all three characters simply bowed in prayer as they kneel in front of the tomb during the song. They exit at the end as Narrator comes to the front.)

NARRATOR: What a privilege it was for those who came to the tomb on that first, glorious Easter morning. Crushed beneath the weight of hopelessness and despair, their burdens were lifted, and hope abounded when they beheld their king in all His radiant splendor. Thankful, forgiven, and restored they quickly spread the news of the empty tomb and the promise it contained. Just think of the indescribable joy they would have missed if they had stayed away. And aren't you glad Jesus chose real people—people we can identify with—to carry His message? For who among us has not felt plagued by anger, selfish desires, confusion over worries in this life, doubts about our faith, and fears about tomorrow? But because of Christ and His sacrifice we can put all those demons to rest and come before His throne of grace and mercy. The nails plus one cross equals forgiveness. That's the message from the cross. And one empty tomb equals victory over death. That's the promise from the tomb, the promise that death is not final and that fearing death is not necessary if we believe in Christ. Jesus said, "Trust in God; trust also in me. In my Father's house are many rooms; if it were not so, I would have told you. I am going there to prepare a place for you. And if I go and prepare a place for you, I will come back and take you to be with me that you also may be where I am" (John 14:1-3). Is there any greater assurance than to know that one day the eastern sky will split open and Jesus Christ, our Savior, will appear on the clouds in all His glory and take us home with Him? Because He lives, we too shall live! May the power of the cross and the promise from the tomb fill your hearts with joy as we celebrate our hope as Christians on this awesome resurrection morning! He is risen, He is risen indeed!

Rocking Easter

V. Louise Cunningham

Characters:
DON, Senior citizen
HELEN, Senior citizen
JOE, Neighbor
STEVE, Jogger
TIFFANY, Steve's daughter

Costumes: Contemporary

Props: Two rocking chairs on an empty stage, a screen or white sheet for backdrop, slides or a cross and backdrop of an empty tomb, nails, hammer.

Setting: Don is enamored with the wonder of rocking chairs and sits on his front porch and visits with neighbors. Each character rocks at varying speeds and rhythms. Slides or using a bright light and shadows to silhouette actors acting out the crucifixion scene and the empty tomb can be used.

Scene 1

Don is sitting in one of the rocking chairs, rocking.

DON: That man who wrote the book was surely a wise man.
HELEN *(entering):* Whom are you talking to?
DON: Just myself. I was thinking out loud about that old book I read. The author certainly had the right idea. Many of the world's problems would be solved if everyone would just fit some rocking chair time in his life. These chairs were the best investment we ever made. Sit down and rock with me.
HELEN: I don't know, I have a lot of things to do in the house before tomorrow. It is Easter Sunday. *(Sits down in the other rocking chair and starts rocking.)* These are comfortable chairs.

DON: I thought you wouldn't have to do anything since we are "so mature" and the children are doing most of the dinner fixing.

HELEN: They are fixing dinner but there are still things that need to be done in the house.

DON: There is always something we should be doing. I'm content to wait and let the grandsons bring in the extra table and chairs from the garage tomorrow.

HELEN: I'm afraid the longer I sit here the harder it will be to get motivated again.

DON: That's the beauty of rocking. It relaxes you.

HELEN: I was thinking about the pageant that we saw earlier this week. People haven't changed; we still face all the same problems today: jealousy, betrayal, busyness, dinners.

DON: It was an excellent presentation. The temple officials were strongly acted and it brought home how jealous they were and fearful of their jobs.

HELEN: The thing that I was impressed with was the fact about how they did everything illegally with their night trials and trumped up charges.

DON: I would have liked to have been there when the guards talked to the temple officials after Jesus was crucified and said that the body was gone. I bet they did a lot of running around to find money to bribe the guards into saying the disciples stole the body of Jesus.

HELEN: Well, as nice as this is, I need to do something with dinner before the news comes on. Aren't you going to come in? *(Stands up.)*

DON: No, I believe I'll just sit out here a spell and rock.

HELEN: You can bring your chair in the house. *(Leaves.)*

DON: It will take her a while before she gets the drift of doing nothing but sitting and rocking, and it works better out here on the porch. *(He continues to rock.)*

Scene 2

Don is still rocking. Joe enters and walks by.

JOE: Enjoying the night air?

DON: Sure am. Why don't you come up and sit with me?

JOE *(looks at chair and sits down):* Nice chair. Are you sure its safe? Where's the seat belt? *(Looking down at sides of chair.)*

DON: I think you'll be all right if you just rock gently. How's it going with you? You look like you lost your best friend.

JOE: I guess you could say that. Today I found out that the person I thought was a good friend betrayed me. I'm having a hard time dealing with that.

DON: You are certainly not the first to be betrayed.

JOE: Guess you are thinking of the Easter pageant and Judas.

DON: I guess I was. Judas was one of Jesus' disciples for three years.

JOE: That's what makes it so hard when you are close to someone and you think he has the same goals and ideas you have.

DON: Imagine the pain Jesus knew living with a man who He knew would betray Him. Jesus suffered more on earth than we will ever be able to imagine.

JOE: He came to earth to show the nation of Israel what God was like and those very people rejected Him.

DON: It is amazing how even to the end, Jesus gave him a chance to do the right thing.

JOE: I hear you. I need to go talk to my friend and see if part of what happened may have been my fault, and if so, I will ask forgiveness and then leave it for God to work in the situation.

DON: Something like that. Jesus said, "Father, forgive them, for they do not know what they are doing" (Luke 23:34, *NIV*).

JOE: You know, this is really restful, sitting and rocking. I just may have to get me a chair. Best get home to the wife and kids. Thanks for listening.

DON: Anytime.

(Joe leaves. Don continues to sit and rock. Steve enters, jogging and carrying a towel in his belt.)

DON: Come up and sit a spell.

STEVE *(jogging in place):* Hi, Don. I'm out for my jog and I have another mile to go.

DON: Come and rock. That will give you exercise.

STEVE: You're kidding. *(Jogs up to the empty chair.)*

DON: It's okay. You can sit.

STEVE: I jog mostly to release stress from everything.

DON: Then a rocking chair is just the thing.

(Steve sits down and mops his face with the towel.)

DON: I've been reading up on rocking chairs. Pretty fascinating stuff. Years ago a doctor wrote that it is good for older people because it gently exercises arm and leg muscles. It also helps avert blood clots, arteriosclerosis, dropsy, and other old-age ailments.

STEVE: Well, it certainly seems a lot easier than jogging.

HELEN: Don, can you come here for a minute?

DON: Excuse me. She is all in a tizzy about Easter dinner. Just keep rocking and I'll be back. *(Leaves.)*

(Steve looks around and gets in a rhythm of rocking.)

TIFFANY: Hi, Dad. Why are you sitting on Mr. G's porch?

STEVE: I'm rocking and waiting for Mr. G to come back out.

TIFFANY: Mom said I could ride my bike to the corner to wait for you. *(Puts her bike down and goes to stand by the rocking chair.)* May I sit in this chair?

STEVE: Until Mr. G comes back out and then he'll want his chair.

TIFFANY: How do you make it go? *(Her feet can't touch the floor.)*

STEVE: You put your feet on the floor. I see the problem. Your feet don't reach the floor. Why don't you come and sit on my lap?

(Tiffany goes over and climbs in her dad's lap.)

STEVE *(rocking):* This is a pretty good way to relieve stress.

DON *(entering):* Helen doesn't need any more help. So, did I hear you talking about stress?

STEVE: I was telling Tiffany that rocking was better than running to relieve stress.

DON: So you must have a pretty full plate of activities.

STEVE: Yes, with working, family, keeping up a house, church activities, they all add up and I do get stressed out. I really worked up a sweat before I sat down. *(Wipes his forehead with his towel.)*

DON: Seeing your towel made me think of loving service and how Jesus washed His disciples' feet.

STEVE: That really must have caused the disciples to think. They were all so busy getting ready for the Passover, everybody was ready to sit back and let someone else take the part of a servant. Nobody was humble enough, except Jesus, to take a towel and stoop down to wash everyone's feet.

DON: Sometimes we get stressed out because we are doing someone else's job.

STEVE: At least you have an advantage. You are retired and don't have to add at least forty hours of work to your schedule.

DON: Sometimes I feel busier than when I was working and of course my physical limits have changed. It takes me longer to do things than it used to. I have to pray and figure out where God wants me to use the towel He has given me.

STEVE: After hearing that, I guess I should evaluate and check my goals.

TIFFANY: What does that mean?

STEVE: That means figuring out what is most important in life.

TIFFANY: Does that mean it is time to go home for dinner?

STEVE: It sure does. Do you think you can beat me home?

TIFFANY: I'd rather ride beside you.

STEVE: Good idea. Good night, Don. Thanks for setting me straight.

DON: Come back anytime and rock with me.

STEVE: We will do that, won't we, Tiffany?

TIFFANY: Yes, Dad. Pretty soon I'll be tall enough that my feet will touch the floor.

(Steve and Tiffany exit. Don continues to rock and falls asleep.)

HELEN *(entering):* Don? Oh, I guess he fell asleep. No hurry, I'll ask him later. *(Leaves.)*

Scene 3

The congregation sings the first two verses of "Were You There?" During the singing, the scene of soldiers and three crosses can be shown. You can also use shadows of the action around the cross on a sheet, or slides of the crucifixion scene, or actors. Sound effects of nails being driven into wood also would be effective.

DON *(rocking violently):* No! Stop! He's innocent. I'm the one who has sinned! *(Leans forward and hides his head in his hands.)*

(Someone sings "Beneath the Cross of Jesus" as the cross and a figure kneeling in front of it is shown.)

HELEN: Whom are you talking to? *(She sits in the rocking chair.)*
DON *(shaking his head):* No one, I must have been talking in my dream.
HELEN: It must have been some dream.
DON: It was. It was like I was right there when they crucified Jesus. I remember saying it was my sins that put Him there and I was trying to stop the Roman soldiers.
HELEN: At least the crucifixion isn't the end of the story.
DON: You mean I should go back to sleep and finish the dream?
HELEN: You know what I mean. Because Jesus died on the cross for us, we have hope.
DON: That's true, and that is what Easter is all about. Sometimes I wonder if our grandchildren understand it all. In the dream, I felt like I was the only one at the cross. I was kneeling. What's incredible is that Jesus can and did forgive all my sins. It's no wonder I felt as if I had lost my heavy burden.
HELEN: I liked the way the pageant ended at church.
DON: It was very moving, showing the picture of the empty tomb and singing "Because He Lives."
HELEN: That really made it clear that Jesus overcame death and is alive. Then when we sang "He Lives" it showed how we can live for Christ each day.

(Phone rings.)

HELEN: I'll get it. It must be one of our girls. They said they'd call before they came over with some of the food for tomorrow. *(Leaves.)*

DON *(continuing to rock):* You know, Lord, these chairs must be the best investment we ever made. It is great to be able to rock and talk with neighbors and to pray for them. I remember Joe and his feeling of betrayal. You, Lord, can really understand the feeling of betrayal. I wonder if Judas had a rocking chair and time to think, maybe he would never have betrayed You. And I know if Steve spent more time kicking back and talking with You, he would find his stress level lighten.

HELEN: Don, Gloria wants to talk to you.

DON *(standing):* I'll finish our talk later, Lord. *(He pauses and sets the rocking chair to rocking and then exits. Focus lights on the chair rocking.)*

CONGREGATION: "Because He Lives" and "He Lives"

Characters of the Cross

David A. Olds

This presentation is written for older children. Individually, each person enters from the same side of the stage, delivers his part, and then joins the others to form a line at the front. Costumes appropriate to the parts enhance the effect. This presentation would still be effective even if some of the less essential parts could not be filled.

PERSON 1: I am the **crown** that soldiers platted and placed on Jesus' head to mock Him for teaching that He was the King of the Jews. I brought great pain and suffering to the head of Jesus as my thorns cut deep into His scalp. But the crown of thorns has been transformed into a crown of glory.

PERSON 2: I am **Simon**, a Cyrenian. I carried Jesus' cross for Him because He was unable to bear it alone all the way to Calvary. Having the opportunity to serve the One who gave so much to mankind was such a blessing from God.

PERSON 3: I am one of the **nails** driven into the precious hands and feet of Jesus—those same hands that tenderly held children and touched the sick with healing goodness. Those same feet carried the Good News to the multitudes. I, too, brought great pain and suffering to Jesus during the hours before His death. My scars remain in His hands and feet forever, but are now scars of victory.

PERSON 4: I am **one of the thieves** crucified with Jesus. I, like many sinners, had the opportunity to accept Him as my Savior, but my heart was too hard; so I died a sinner and forever lost the opportunity for salvation.

PERSON 5: I am the **other thief** crucified beside Jesus. I, too, had a hard heart at first; and, just as many others, I mocked Jesus while He was dying on the cross. But soon I realized that He was no ordinary man and certainly not a criminal. When I understood that He was truly the Son of God, I accepted Him as my Savior and went with Him the day we died. I am so thankful I made the right choice.

PERSON 6: I am one of the **chief priests** who mocked Jesus. It seemed like the right thing to do at the time. Why, even the scribes and elders were mocking Him. But now I know I was wrong and that I am totally responsible for rejecting Jesus. No one else can be blamed; no one else can be responsible for my terrible mistake. Oh, how happy I am I will get another chance.

PERSON 7: I am the **garments** and the **coat** of Jesus. The soldiers made four parts of the garments and divided them among themselves; but His coat was seamless, very special, so instead of tearing it into parts, they cast lots to decide which soldier got the coat. They didn't even realize at the time that they were fulfilling a prophecy that these very things would take place. God changed a negative into a positive by this confirmation of prophecy.

PERSON 8: I am **Mary Magdalene**. I was one of the women who watched Jesus die on the cross. Words cannot tell you how it broke my heart to see my Master go through so much pain and suffering. He had been so good to me. Not only did He free me from the seven demons that had controlled my life; but He treated me as a real person. Jesus truly loved me.

PERSON 9: I am the **sign** that Pilate wrote and placed on the cross. I was written in Hebrew, Greek, and Latin. Some of the chief priests tried to persuade Pilate to word me to read that Jesus merely said He was King of the Jews. But Pilate refused to take their advice and wrote instead: "Jesus of Nazareth, the King of the Jews."

PERSON 10: I am **Mary** the mother of Jesus. I felt all the grief and suffering a mother feels for her son when he is being killed, killed slowly by crucifixion on a cross, a punishment normally reserved for criminals. My Son was innocent. He did only good His entire life. At the cross, I remembered rocking Him in my arms when He was a baby, and how I daydreamed of His growing up to become a man and all the joy that would bring me. His death and the suffering He endured before His crucifixion were horrible. I know now that He had to suffer and die on the cross so that all of mankind may be saved; but He was still my baby, and His death hurt me so.

PERSON 11: I am the **spear** that pierced Jesus' side. There was nothing special about me before a soldier used me to puncture Jesus' side to make sure He was dead. I was just another piece of metal that had been shaped into an instrument of death. But, unknown to me at the time, I became an instrument of eternal life that day.

PERSON 12: I am **John**, known most often as the disciple whom Jesus loved. My close relationship with my Savior led Him to tell me, when He was dying on the cross, to take care of His mother. I cannot express what I felt at the time; my emotions were a mixture of pain and joy. I was happy and honored that our close relationship led Him to tell me to take care of His mother, but my heart was heavy as a shield at the same time because my Master and friend was dying.

PERSON 13: I am the **cross** used to crucify the Savior of the world. I was made from a simple tree, and at first there was nothing especially different about me; my appearance was the same as all the other crosses used for crucifixions. Ah, but eventually I became the symbol of salvation and through the years have been recognized by billions of people as the cross that brought true deliverance to the world.

PERSON 14: I am **Joseph of Arimathea**, a rich man, a just man, a disciple of Jesus. Following Jesus' death, I asked Pilate to let me bury Jesus' body. Eventually, he consented and I wrapped the body in clean linen and laid it in my own new tomb. I placed a huge stone at the entrance before leaving.

PERSON 15: I am **Jesus**, the Son of God, the Lily of the Valley, the Prince of Peace, your eternal hope. I am the holy lamb that was slain on the cross of Calvary for the sins of all people. I arose and now I am alive. I knock at the door of every person's heart and ask him to let me come in. I sacrificed my life to give the world eternal life and a peace within that surpasses all understanding. Am I living in your heart?

ALL: *(Close by singing an appropriate Easter song.)*

A Gift for Mom

V. Louise Cunningham

Two sisters are talking about the upcoming Mother's Day and what present to get for their mother.

Characters:
LISA, the younger sister
JODY, the older sister

Props: Phone, table, chairs

Time: Contemporary

LISA: I don't know what to get Mom for Mother's Day. She has everything she needs; and if she doesn't, she goes out and buys it.

JODY: Time.

LISA: It's about 3:30. Why?

JODY: No, Mom wants time as a gift.

LISA: What do you mean? I don't understand.

JODY: You aren't listening to her. At her age she doesn't need or want things. She is trying to get rid of some of what she has. When you see her, doesn't she ask what you would like?

LISA: Yes, and I tell her to enjoy her things.

JODY: Like I said, she would like something more valuable. Time. She would like us to give her an hour or so a week on a regular basis.

LISA: You know how busy I am. I'm barely keeping my head above water now. During the week I have to fix dinner, make sure the kids do their homework, and usually I have to run them somewhere. Saturday and Sundays I have to catch up on my housework.

JODY: It is tough but if you really wanted to give her something special, you could give her coupons for going shopping, having her over for dinner, meeting her for lunch.

LISA: Usually I don't know what I'm fixing for dinner, or we eat in such a rush to get to church or something. Besides, coupons are kid stuff.

JODY: You don't think Mom would rather have a cup of tea with you and hear about what your family is doing in person rather than on the phone? When you go shopping you can ask her if she wants to go with you. That has two benefits. She will feel like she is part of your family and she gets to spend time with you.

LISA: It is easier for you to do that stuff with her. Your kids are grown and not living at home anymore.

JODY: That's true. I also know that when one of my kids invites me to go shopping with her or asks us to eat dinner with her family, it is a wonderful gift. *(Pauses.)* You look like you are in deep thought.

LISA: You know, I have some volunteers helping me and I always pick up some nice gifts for them. One year, one of them said to me that she didn't need gifts because she enjoyed helping. But she said when things slowed down for me, she would like to have breakfast or lunch with me.

JODY: So did you do that?

LISA: No, it was easier to buy a gift than find time. But now I think I hear what you are saying.

JODY: Well, I've got to run, so I'll be in touch about what to bring on Mother's Day. *(She leaves.)*

LISA: Okay. Great. *(Goes to the phone.)* Hi, Mom, this is Lisa. *(Pause.)* I know it isn't my usual day to call but I was wondering if you would like to go shopping with me tomorrow? I need to pick up a few things and then maybe we could have lunch. *(Pause.)* You would? Great, I can pick you up about 9:30.

Thanks, Mom

Lillian Robbins

A reading for an adult.

Mom, you are endowed with the wisdom of Solomon, the patience of Job, and the love of the Father above.

You convinced me to take baths when I'd rather play in the mud, and you taught me to play with care instead of streaking uninhibited across the street.

You insisted on healthy eating habits rather than permitting me to stuff myself with those good, gooey sweets.

When I was sick and couldn't run and play, you read books to me, and when I was lonely you were my favorite partner in games. I was never sure which brought the healing to my injuries, those fancy bandages you always had ready or your tender touch and comforting words.

You banished my fears with assurance that dark would not hurt me and my place in life would be secure.

You were thrilled when I succeeded in any endeavor and joy sprang from your heart when I was happy. But you cried barrels of tears when problems arose and life was difficult for both of us.

Your life was like a roller coaster with its ups and down, heights of elation and valleys of depression, often attributed to being my mother.

Through it all you gave me stability with love and discipline metered out in proper proportions.

I have always marveled at the strength with which you provided roots in my life and then so calmly gave me wings to fly away from the nest. Though you experienced a feeling of emptiness, you never let me see your loneliness.

Now I'm an adult and just want to say again, I love you. If I could have searched the world over, I never would have found a better mom than you. Thanks for being my mom and being so special in every way.

Umbrellas
V. Louise Cunningham

Characters: LORI AND JULIA

Props: Umbrellas, including a travel umbrella and a big golf umbrella, some open and placed decoratively around, and some in stands.

Time: Contemporary

LORI: Umbrellas!

JULIA: Hello. Earth to Lori. We were talking about husbands and our attitudes.

LORI: I am on the same subject as you are. *(Picks up umbrella and opens it.)*

JULIA: Hey, isn't it bad luck to open an umbrella inside?

LORI: I think it's okay in a store. I just wanted to make a point. This little travel umbrella won't do a lot of good in a big rainstorm. It may keep your face dry, but not your arms, because it is so small.

JULIA *(picks up an umbrella):* I really like this one with the cats on it. They sure make them now with all kinds of things: flowers, birds, cats, dogs.

LORI: This isn't very fancy but it is larger and will do the job.

JULIA: If you want one that does more, how about this jumbo size?

LORI: That would be a good illustration for a good husband and father.

JULIA: There you go again. I don't see the point.

LORI *(picks up a big umbrella and holds it over her head):* A husband is like an umbrella.

JULIA: Okay. Men come in all heights and widths and have different interests.

LORI: God placed men so that they could be shields of protection around women and children, like an umbrella. *(Holds open umbrella out to the side so it isn't over her head.)* If women and children don't allow men to cover them, they are going to get hurt or wet.

JULIA: So it is kind of like a shield that the Bible talks about. God says that He is a shield, but if we don't stay behind Him, then we are going to get hurt.

LORI: Let me try and give you an example. We had a windstorm a few years ago and our tottering fence blew down.

JULIA: I remember. The fence kept your little dog in and your husband was out of town.

LORI: Even though Duane was out of town, I could call him and let him make the exact decision of what to do. Then I called the insurance people and so forth.

JULIA: I guess I know what you mean, even though some women are more efficient at organizing and seeing a problem.

LORI: How many times have you taken the car in to be fixed or had a repairman out to your house and been treated unfairly by those men? Sometimes the men treat women as if they don't know anything and sometimes take advantage of them.

JULIA: Yet, if my husband is with me, the treatment is totally different.

LORI: Fair or not, that's the way it is.

JULIA: And it would be the same way for our children. Their father protects them and cares for them like an umbrella protects them from the rain.

LORI: That is true. So what are your kids going to get their father for Father's Day?

JULIA: An umbrella, of course. *(Picks up an umbrella and twirls it.)* A big umbrella like this one that we will all fit under. *(Puts down smaller umbrella for the biggest one.)*

A Letter to Dad

Lillian Robbins

A special reading for Father's Day.

Hi Dad,

I apologize for getting this letter to you late, but I have been so busy lately, I just didn't find time to write. I meant to call you on Father's Day but my work takes so much time. I have many obligations to attend business meetings and social activities. But tonight I didn't have anything else to do, so I'm writing to you.

Oh, dear! Dad, what did I just say in this letter? That when nothing else demands my attention, I think about you. How thoughtless I have been. I'm sorry, a thousand times I'm sorry. There is no business deal or social function important enough to take your place in my heart.

How can I forget those wonderful days of my youth? I can see you now, sitting at your desk late at night. When I crept down the stairs and opened your door, you asked, "What is it, Child? What do you need?" You weren't too busy to stop in the middle of your work to sit with me at the kitchen table while I sipped a glass of milk. Tucking me in bed again, you said good night and resumed your work.

I remember when you left work to take me fishing or to the old swimming hole in the creek, which happened to be so much more fun than the city pool. How about the days we played catch and you showed me just the way to hold the ball for a good pitch.

I remember when you canceled plans for a trip so you could drive me to camp. I wouldn't go with anyone else.

At times I thought you were far behind the times, and I wondered why you didn't wise up. When you grounded me, I was angry. I thought you were being mean but now I can only say, "Thanks, Pop." Without your loving me enough to steer me in the right direction, I never would have been successful. How can a kid be so foolish as to think he knows more than his dad?

The person-to-person talk we had when I decided to get married must have been difficult for you. It was a cold December day, and I remember that you were sweating. I was grown up, but I was your little boy, just a little bigger, and about to take one of the most important steps in my life.

Through the years I thought I had to be the best and climb the ladder faster and higher than my competitors if I was going to make you proud of me. Now I know you only wanted me to accomplish what I had the ability to do.

You taught me to love the Lord and my fellowman, and to respect the rights of others. You taught me to be compassionate and to forgive when I had been wronged. Always, your main message was that I should talk to the Lord and follow His guidance.

I wish we could stroll once again through the park where our close communion always served as a balm for weary days. Or maybe we could settle down on the back steps again where you encouraged me and inspired me to seek that which is good. You planted more love seeds in my heart than the flowers in Mom's garden that produced so many beautiful fragrant blossoms.

It is believed that older people can't remember well, but I have just discovered that young people have the same problem. I might not forget where I left the newspaper or if I mailed the check for the telephone bill, but look how I was so preoccupied that I didn't even remember you on Father's Day.

Forgive me for being so lax. God gave me a wonderful blessing when He created me as your child. Thanks, Dad. I really love you, yesterday, today, and all the days to come.

From your imperfect offspring who is still trying to reach the stars that you revealed through your special wisdom and love. In the future, I will not be so negligent to say, "I love you, Dad."